HEROES OF THE TITANIC

Written by Anne Marie Welsh
Illustrated by Ryan Hobson

SCHOLASTIC

Copyright © 2011 becker&mayer! LLC

Published by Tangerine Press, an imprint of Scholastic Inc., 557 Broadway, New York, NY 10012; Scholastic Canada Ltd., Markham, Ontario; Scholastic Australia Pty. Ltd, Gosford NSW; Scholastic New Zealand Ltd., Greenmount, Auckland
All rights reserved.

Scholastic and Tangerine Press and associated logos are trademarks of Scholastic Inc.

Heroes of the Titanic is produced by becker&mayer!
11120 NE 33rd Place, Suite 101
Bellevue, WA 98004
www.beckermayer.com

Written by Anne Marie Welsh
Edited by Betsy Henry Pringle
Designed by Sarah Baynes
Design Assistance by Rosanna Brockley
Illustrated by Ryan Hobson
Photo Research by Zena Chew and Katie del Rosario
Facts checked by Dan Janeck
Production management by Jennifer Marx

Printed, manufactured, and assembled in HangZhou, China, December 2011

10 9 8 7 6 5 4 3

ISBN: 978-0-545-37509-2

11117

Cover: portrait of Anna Turja © Titanic Historical Society, Inc.; Jack Thayer crew team photo © University of Pennsylvania Archives; Ruth Becker portrait © no attribution/Wikimedia Commons; Violet Jessop portrait © from Titanic Survivor, Sheridan House Inc./the Collection of Margaret and Mary Meehan. Title page: Titanic at the docks © no attribution/Wikimedia Commons. Pages 4-5: Advertisement © Advertising Archive/Courtesy Everett Collection; Fred Fleet © Harris & Ewing Collection/Library of Congress; antique binoculars © Andrew Buckin/Dreamstime.com; Stower sinking © New York World-Telegram and the Sun Newspaper Photograph Collection/Library of Congress; antique compass © Irochka/Dreamstime.com. Pages 6-7: White star lines building © ilbuscaphotography/iStockphoto; Titanic's grand staircase © White Star Line brochure from 1912, Mary Evans Picture Library/Everett Collection. Pages 10-11: Captain Smith: © Mary Evans Picture Library/Everett Collection; Captain Smith and officers © CSU Archives/Everett Collection; pocket watch © Sergejs Razvodovskis/iStockphoto; iceberg © Mark Evans/iStockphoto. Pages 12-13: reproduction of Titanic menu based upon White Star Lines menu, 1912; gymnasium © Father Browne/Universal Images Group/Premium Archive/Getty Images; first class steward pin © Mary Evans Picture Library/Everett Collection; Thayer yearbook photo and Thayer crew team photo © University of Pennsylvania Archives; 1st class suite and 1st class bathroom © National Museums Northern Ireland, Collection Harland & Wolff, Ulster Folk & Transport Museum. Pages 14-15: Ship propeller © George Grantham Bain Collection/Library of Congress; Collapsible B © Image courtesy of Independence Seaport Museum (Philadelphia, PA), Thayer Family Collection, 1989.033; Thayer sketches © NOAA. Pages 16-17: reproduction of ticket based upon White Star Lines ticket, 1912; 2nd class stateroom © Mary Evans Picture Library/Everett Collection; Ruth Becker portrait © no attribution/Wikimedia Commons; Promenade deck © New York World-Telegram and the Sun Newspaper Photograph Collection/Library of Congress. Pages 18-19: 3rd class advertisement © Mary Evans Picture Library/Everett Collection; portrait of Anna Turja © Titanic Historical Society, Inc.; 3rd class general room © Photograph © National Museums Northern Ireland. Pages 20-21: life vest © cliff1066/Flickr; lifeboats illustration © Bob Thomas/Popperfoto/Getty Images; Survivors on Carpathia © Library of Congress. Pages 22-23: Turkish bath © Mary Evans Picture Library/Everett Collection; Violet Jessop portrait © from Titanic Survivor, Sheridan House Inc./the Collection of Margaret and Mary Meehan; Olympic © Detroit Publishing Company Photograph Collection/Library of Congress; dinner party from movie © 20th Century Fox Film Corp/Everett Collection; antique fan © Margojh/Dreamstime.com. Pages 24-25: Marconi room © John Jenkins/American Museum of Radio and Electricity; Marconi stamp © Steve Mann/Dreamstime.com; Phillips portrait © The National Archives/Photolibrary; Harold Bride © Mirrorpix/Courtesy Everett Collection; Telegrams © Universal Images Group/Premium Archive/Getty Images; British Post Office Morse key © Ian Poole/Dreamstime.com. Pages 26-27: Edwardian fashion © Mary Evans Picture Library/Everett Collection; Andrews portrait © Mary Evans Picture Library/Everett Collection; lifeboats on the Olympic © Library of Congress; drafting compass © Pefkos/shutterstock. Pages 28-29: Molly Brown © George Grantham Bain Collection/Library of Congress; lifeboats (background) © George Grantham Bain Collection/Library of Congress; Countess of Rothes © Universal Images Group/Premium Archive/Getty Images; Lightoller portrait © Illustrated London News Ltd./Everett Collection. Pages 30-31: Suffragettes © Library of Congress; Helen Candee © no attribution/Wikimedia Commons; Molly Brown poster © Everett Collection; Mahala Douglas portrait © Brucemore, Inc., a National Trust Historic Site, Cedar Rapids, Iowa. Pages 34-35: Mailbags © Father Browne/Universal Images Group/Getty Images; antique postcards © Stephanie Phillips/iStockphoto; musicians © Mary Evans Picture Library/Everett Collection; Straus portrait courtesy of Straus Historical Society, Inc. Pages 36-37: William T. Stead portrait © no attribution/Wikimedia Commons; smoking room © William H. Rau/Library of Congress; gloves © Nikolay Pozdeev/Dreamstime.com; John Jacob Astor © George Grantham Bain Collection/Library of Congress; Madeleine Astor © Library of Congress; Captain Smith © Library of Congress. Pages 38-39: Arthur Rostron © George Grantham Bain Collection/Library of Congress; Carpathia © George Grantham Bain Collection/Library of Congress; lifeboat © New York World-Telegram and the Sun Newspaper Photograph Collection/Library of Congress. Pages 40-41: Lifeboat 2 © New York World-Telegram and the Sun Newspaper Photograph Collection/Library of Congress; Eva Hart portrait © Everett Collection; Collapsible D © National Archives and Records Administration – Northeast Region (New York); Captain Rostron with Marjory Sweetheart © Everett; Survivors on Carpathia © Hulton Archive/Getty Images; Statue of Liberty © Library of Congress. Pages 42-43: Newsboy © Hulton Archive/Getty Images; New York Herald © Library of Congress; Harold Bride © Library of Congress; crowd awaiting survivors © George Grantham Bain Collection/Library of Congress. Pages 44-45: Smith portrait © Harris & Ewing Collection/Library of Congress; gavel © Ron Chapple Studios/Dreamstime.com; Waldorf Astoria © Detroit Publishing Co./Library of Congress; Bruce Ismay © no attribution/Wikimedia Commons; Ismay testifies © Library of Congress; Molly Brown and Captain Rostron © Library of Congress. Pages 46-47: Robert Ballard © Emory Kristof/National Geographic; painting © Pierre Mion/National Geographic Society/Corbis; bow © Emory Kristof/National Geographic; dishes © Ralph White/Corbis. Pages 48-49: Widener Library © Will Hart/Flickr; Memorial © Library of Congress.

CONTENTS

The Titanic Tragedy

When the White Star Line ship RMS *Titanic* set sail from Southampton, England, on April 10, 1912, it was the largest, most luxurious ship to ever sail the ocean. Passengers included millionaires returning to America from European vacations, immigrants seeking a better life, and a crew of nearly 900 men and women. Four days into the *Titanic*'s maiden voyage, it struck an iceberg and sank into the icy Atlantic Ocean. More than 2,200 people were aboard—only 705 survived.

The *Titanic*'s fateful voyage is a tale of opulence, tragedy, and heroism. The stories of those who survived—and those who perished—remind us that life can take unexpected turns that we can't control. These stories also show that, when times are at their most difficult, each of us has the opportunity and the capacity to become a hero.

TITANIC

The World's Largest Liner

WHITE STAR LINE

SOUTHAMPTON ~ NEW YORK
VIA CHERBOURG & QUEENSTOWN

Lookout
Frederick Fleet

Although there may have been binoculars aboard the *Titanic*, the lookouts could not find them.

PROLOGUE

April 14, 1912. The air that Sunday night was cold and clear. The ocean's surface, smooth as glass, reflected a moonless sky sparkling with stars. Shivering in the crow's nest, the highest lookout point on RMS *Titanic*, Lookout Frederick Fleet wished he had a pair of binoculars. He had spotted something strange ahead—a dark mass looming up from the sea.

After dining in the first-class restaurant and sharing stories with a new friend, young Jack Thayer was preparing for bed. Molly Brown, a fun-loving socialite from Denver, Colorado, was reading a book in her first-class cabin.

At 11:40 p.m., Fleet's fear came into focus. He banged the alarm bell and telephoned the bridge. "Iceberg right ahead!" On the bridge, the first officer gave the order to reverse the engines and turn the ship. As the *Titanic* slowly turned, the submerged part of the iceberg scraped the ship's side, slicing into the hull.

In her second-class cabin, Ruth Becker's mother woke—had the ship's engines stopped? Anna Turja and Minnie Coutts, passengers in third class, felt a sharp jolt.

Jack Thayer noticed that the air coming through an open porthole had suddenly grown colder. Lookout Fleet heard "a grinding noise." And night baker Walter Belford felt the ship sway, as a pan of his just-baked rolls clattered to the floor.

Men in smoking rooms continued playing cards. Other passengers, including children, slept.

Stillness and silence fell over the *Titanic* shortly before midnight. The ship's enormous coal-fired engines stopped. The greatest ship ever built glided to a standstill in the cold, dark waters of the North Atlantic.

Twenty minutes later, the ship's captain talked quietly with Thomas Andrews. Andrews was the Irishman who had helped design the *Titanic*. By then, the two men knew the worst. Six of the watertight compartments below were open to the sea and filling with water. The ship was doomed. It would not be long before the *Titanic* would sink.

In the 140 minutes before that happened, heroic efforts of the crew and many passengers helped 705 people survive. More than twice that number died, many bravely.

Boys and girls, men and women became heroes that fateful night. They stayed calm, offered comfort, and acted selflessly. When the "unsinkable" ship plunged more than two miles to the bottom of the sea, their names became part of its legend.

These are their stories.

THE SHIP OF DREAMS

The owners of the White Star Line were worried. A rival British company, the Cunard Line, had launched two ships that were the talk of London. The Cunard ships crossed the ocean in just five days, a record. How could the White Star Line and its Harland and Wolff shipbuilders compete?

In a London mansion during the summer of 1907, two businessmen found a way. They agreed to build three giant ships. Each would be bigger and more elegant than Cunard's *Lusitania* and *Mauritania*. The White Star owners would call their massive passenger liners the *Olympic*, *Titanic*, and *Gigantic*.

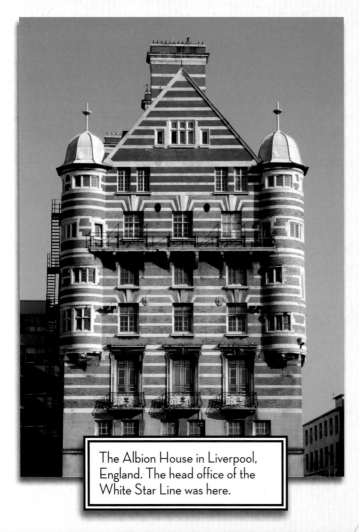

The Albion House in Liverpool, England. The head office of the White Star Line was here.

Work Begins on the Titanic and Olympic

Six thousand shipbuilders began work at Harland and Wolff's shipyard in Belfast, Ireland. Two years later, the *Titanic* towered above them, a huge sleek hull, its steel plates fastened by millions of rivets. Thousands of people came to watch it glide into the water, for the *Titanic* was the largest ship ever built.

For ten more months, workers "fitted out" the ship. They added coal-fired boilers, propellers, a generator for electricity, and glass portholes, called sidelights. Next came four elevators, floorboards, walls, ceilings, pipes, and wires.

First-class passenger Mrs. Mahala Douglas remembered the ship as "so luxurious, so steady, so immense, and such a marvel of mechanism that one could not believe he was on a boat—and there the danger lay. We had smooth seas, clear starlit nights, fresh favoring winds; nothing to mar our pleasure."

Built-in Elegance

First-class bedrooms and parlors were decorated to resemble rooms in mansions and palaces. Ornately carved wood and a marble fireplace warmed the first-class lounge. A beautiful glass and wrought iron dome soared above an elegant grand staircase.

Dining saloons for second- and third-class passengers were better than those on other ships. Still, those in first class would have the most choices. Aside from the opulent dining saloon, where the wealthy would enjoy 11-course meals seated amid leaded glass and classical statues, they might eat at the small, deluxe à la carte restaurant. Diners at the Café Parisien would be treated to ocean views from huge windows.

Titanic's grand staircase.

Titanic by the Numbers

These numbers will help you imagine how immense the *Titanic* really was.

PEOPLE

- 2,207 on board; *Titanic* could hold 3,547 fully loaded
- 1,315 passengers
- 892 crew members

SIZE

- 4 city blocks long
- 11 stories tall from hull to funnel tops
- 53,000 tons (48,080 metric tons)
- 9 decks

POWER

- 29 boilers released steam to turn the propellers
- 162 coal-fired furnaces heated the water in the boilers
- 600 tons (562 t) of coal burned each day, shoveled in by men called "stokers"
- 2 side propellers, each 23 feet (7 m) wide, pushed the ship
- 1 center propeller, 16 feet (4.8 m) wide, pushed and steered
- 28 miles per hour top speed; in nautical measure, 24 "knots"

FOOD	WEIGHT/QUANTITY
Fresh Meat	75,000 pounds (34,000 kg)
Fresh Fish	11,000 pounds (4,990 kg)
Bacon/Ham	7,500 pounds (3,400 kg)
Poultry	25,000 pounds (11,340 kg)
Potatoes	80,000 pounds (36,290 kg)
Milk	1,500 gallons (5,678 l)
Butter	6,000 pounds (2,720 kg)
Apples	36,000
Eggs	40,000
Cigars	8,000
SERVICE ITEMS	**AMOUNT**
China	57,600 pieces
Glasses	29,000
Cutlery	44,000
Linens	196,000

Other choices for first-class passengers included the Verandah Café and Palm Court, both decorated like the gardens of English country houses. Wicker furniture, plants, and trellises would make diners feel they were seated outdoors.

No expense was spared. A smoking room for men in first class featured stained-glass windows and mahogany panels inlaid with mother of pearl. A reading room with delicate furniture was designed for women passengers in first class.

Even the second-class smoking room was fitted to look like an exclusive men's club. Immigrants in third class would be able to share their hopes while sitting on benches on the stern deck, which was open to the sea.

The Dream Begins

The *Olympic* was launched first. When the *Titanic* set sail the following year, it was called the "ship of dreams." As the massive liner embarked on its maiden voyage, headlines said the amazing ship was "unsinkable." The owners of the White Star Line were no longer worried.

INTERIOR OF THE TITANIC

1. 1st-class baggage
2. 1st-class cabins
3. 1st-class dining room
4. 1st-class enclosed promenade
5. 1st-class lounge
6. 1st-class private promenade
7. 1st-class reception room
8. 1st-class smoking room
9. 2nd-class cabins
10. 2nd-class dining room
11. 3rd-class cabins
12. 3rd-class cabins
13. 3rd-class dining room
14. 3rd-class galley
15. 3rd-class general room
16. Aft well deck
17. À la carte restaurant and Café Parisien

18. Boiler rooms
19. Bridge
20. Cargo hold
21. Coal bins
22. Crow's nest
23. Docking bridge
24. Forecastle deck
25. Foremast
26. Forward well deck
27. Funnel
28. Grand staircase
29. Gymnasium
30. Hospital
31. Kitchen
32. Mail room
33. Marconi room
34. Stern deck

35. Post office
36. Propellers
37. Reciprocating engine room
38. Rudder
39. Swimming pool
40. Turbine engine room
41. Turkish baths
42. Verandah Café and Palm Court
43. Wireless antenna
44. Anchor crane

Boat Deck

A Deck

B Deck

C Deck

D Deck

E Deck

F Deck

TITANIC

CAPTAIN EDWARD J. SMITH
The Millionaires' Captain

The Voyage Begins

Captain Edward J. Smith had a lot to feel happy about. He was commanding a majestic ship on its maiden voyage, the sea was calm, and they were making good time. In fact, they might even reach New York ahead of schedule. After 50 years at sea (37 years as a captain), Smith was the White Star Line's most experienced officer. He was such a favorite of the wealthy passengers who traveled between Europe and the United States that he was known as the Millionaires' Captain.

"I never saw a wreck and have never been wrecked, nor was I ever in any predicament that threatened to end in disaster of any sort."

—Captain Smith, Commander of the *Titanic,* in an interview in 1907

Iceberg Reports

At about 9:00 a.m. on Sunday, April 14, a wireless message was received from SS *Caronia*. The message reported: "bergs, growlers, and field ice" ahead. The captain showed the message to Second Officer Charles Lightoller, who posted it in the chartroom at about 1:00 p.m.

Throughout the day, the wireless operators received a number of warnings telling them that the *Titanic* was steaming toward an ice field. At about 6:00 p.m., Captain Smith altered the ship's course 10 miles south, perhaps hoping to avoid the ice ahead. He wasn't particularly worried. He believed his new ship could survive a collision with an iceberg. The captain then went to a dinner party being held in his honor in the ship's elegant à la carte restaurant. The party was hosted by George and Eleanor Widener, a wealthy American couple.

Four of the *Titanic*'s officers, including First Officer William Murdoch (far left) and Captain Smith (far right).

Moving Toward Danger

...ter that evening, Captain Smith excused himself from ...e party and walked to the bridge. He ordered the ...okouts and officers on duty to keep a sharp watch. The ...mperature had plunged from 43 to 33 degrees in two ...urs—a possible sign the ship was approaching ice. It ...as a moonless night, so the officers would not have the ...dvantage of moonlight reflecting off ice in their path. ...nd the sea was calm, so they would not see the white ...am that formed at the base of an iceberg when waves ...oke against it. Captain Smith then retired to his cabin, ...aving Officer Lightoller in charge.

The Titanic Hits an Iceberg

At 10:00 p.m., Lightoller turned the watch over to First Officer William Murdoch. At 11:00 p.m., the nearby SS *Californian* radioed *Titanic*'s wireless operator Jack Phillips. "Say, old man," the operator said, "we are surrounded by ice and stopped." Exhausted and overworked, Phillips impatiently told the *Californian*'s operator to "Shut up!"

No one on the *Titanic*, it seemed, understood the magnitude of the danger ahead.

At 11:40 p.m., Frederick Fleet's frantic call from the crow's nest reached the bridge. Seemingly from nowhere, an enormous wall of ice appeared in front of the *Titanic*. Murdoch ordered the ship to turn, but the submerged portion of the iceberg grazed the *Titanic*'s starboard side, slicing small holes in the hull.

Captain Smith was on the bridge within minutes, but all his years of experience had not prepared him for this moment. Water was pouring into the boiler rooms below, filling the hulls and sinking the "unsinkable" *Titanic*.

Icebergs

An iceberg is a large mass of free-floating polar glacier ice. Small icebergs are called "growlers." Nearly 90 percent of an iceberg lies below the waterline. Although no one knows for sure how large the *Titanic*'s iceberg was, eyewitness accounts report it was as high as 100 feet and as long as 400 feet.

FIRST ★ CLASS

R.M.S. "TITANIC."
April 14, 1912

FIRST CLASS DINNER.

Hors D'Oeuvre Variès

Oysters

Consomme Olga   Cream of Barley

Salmon, Mousseline Sauce, Cucumber

Filet Mignons Lili

Sauté of Chicken Lyonnaise

Vegetable Marrow Farcie

Lamb, Mint Sauce

Roast Duckling, Apple Sauce

Sirloin of Beef Chateau Potatoes

Green Peas   Creamed Carrots

Boiled Rice

Parmentier & Boiled New Potatoes

Punch Romaine

Roast Squab & Cress

Red Burgundy

Cold Asparagus   Vinaigrette

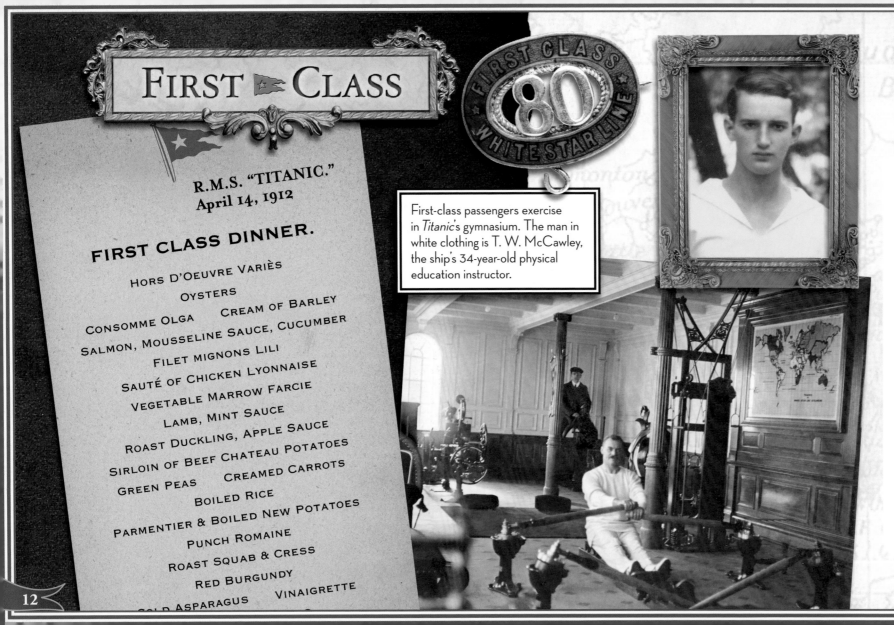

First-class passengers exercise in *Titanic*'s gymnasium. The man in white clothing is T. W. McCawley, the ship's 34-year-old physical education instructor.

JACK THAYER
The Leap That Saved His Life

A Floating Palace

Seventeen-year-old Jack Thayer boarded the *Titanic* with his parents, a wealthy couple from Philadelphia. As first-class passengers, they had access to the most lavish and expensive area of the ship. First-class passengers could use the gymnasium and the squash court. Other first-class amenities included ornate steam rooms, called Turkish baths, and a swimming pool.

Jack, a clean-cut and athletic boy, slept in a stateroom on C deck near his parents' suite. He spent the first four days of the voyage exploring the *Titanic*. Jack also enjoyed chatting with his friend Harry Widener about books. Both young men loved books; Harry had a 3,500-volume collection of rare first editions, and he was returning to the United States with valuable books he had recently purchased in Europe.

Jack noted that the ship's first-class lounge was modeled on a salon in the French palace at Versailles. The cooling room next to the Turkish baths, with its brightly colored tiles, golden beams, and bronze lamps, looked like a shah's palace.

Jack's New Friend

On Sunday evening, the fourth night of their voyage, Jack's parents dined with Captain Smith in the superexpensive à la carte restaurant. They were all guests of Mr. and Mrs. George Widener, Harry's parents. But Jack ate in the first-class dining saloon. Here, he made a new friend, 29-year-old Milton Long from Springfield, Massachusetts. Milton had exciting stories to tell about his travels. He had even survived a shipwreck in Alaska.

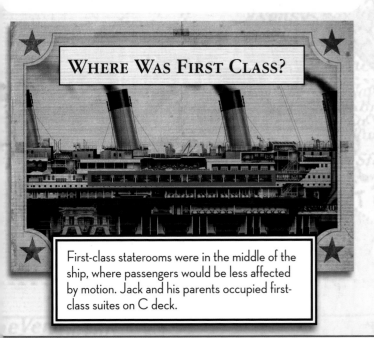

WHERE WAS FIRST CLASS?

First-class staterooms were in the middle of the ship, where passengers would be less affected by motion. Jack and his parents occupied first-class suites on C deck.

The Night Turns Cold

Later, as Jack got ready for bed, he sensed the cold through a porthole and felt the ship sway. The engines stopped. He told his parents he wanted to go out to "see the fun." Outside, Jack was surprised to see pieces of ice on the deck. On a lower deck, some boys were kicking chunks of ice.

About fifteen minutes after the collision, the ship began listing a bit to port (the left side). Jack ran below and found his parents. He put on a suit, two vests, and a life jacket. He placed his overcoat on top of all of this. When they were all dressed, Jack and his parents hurried to the lounge on A deck. By then, women and children were being loaded into lifeboats. While Jack's father secured a place for Mrs. Thayer in Lifeboat 4, Jack caught up with Milton Long.

By this time, all the lifeboats were launched, yet hundreds of people were still on the ship. Jack wanted to slide down ropes that were on the side of the ship and swim to a lifeboat, but Milton wasn't so sure it was a good idea. Jack wouldn't abandon his new friend.

First-class parlor suite.

First-class bathroom.

The *Titanic*'s 350 first-class cabins had telephones, electric heaters, and hot and cold running water. Some had private bathrooms. Many first-class passengers brought their own maids and butlers, who slept in cabins nearby.

Jack Leaps for His Life

The front of the *Titanic,* the bow, sank deeper and deeper into the water. When the bow took a steep dive, the young men had no choice but to jump. Going first, Milton slid close to the side of the ship, was sucked down, and perished.

Thinking quickly, Jack threw off his overcoat and leapt feet first as far as he could from the rail. Later, Jack wrote that he felt he had been *pushed away from the ship by some unseen force.* He hit the water and plunged downward. Surfacing, Jack gasped for air and tried to protect himself from floating debris. Then he stretched out his hand.

Soon after, he felt the cork fender of an overturned lifeboat. Jack wrote, *I looked up and saw some men on the top and asked them to give me a hand. One of them, who was a stoker, helped me up.* Jack had found his way to Collapsible B.

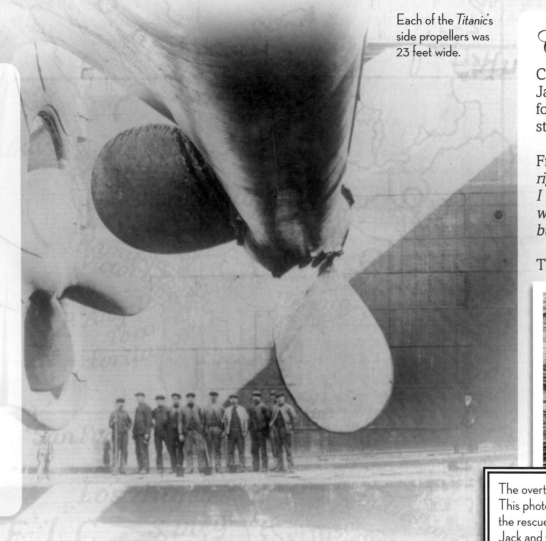

Each of the *Titanic's* side propellers was 23 feet wide.

Collapsible B

Collapsible B had been swept upside down into the frigid waters Jack scrambled onto the overturned boat, where other men had found refuge. Eventually there would be 30 of them struggling to stay alive.

From that position, Jack later wrote, *I looked upwards—we were right underneath the three enormous propellers. For an instant, I thought they were sure to come right down on top of us. Then, with the deadened noise of the bursting of her last few gallant bulkheads, she (the* Titanic*) slid quietly away from us into the se.*

The world's great symbol of progress and wealth simply vanishe

The overturned Collapsible B. This photograph was taken from the rescue ship, the *Carpathia,* after Jack and the others had been taken aboard other lifeboats.

Lifeboat 12

After a grim night, Lifeboats 4 and 12 finally picked up Jack and the others. First-class passenger Algernon Barkworth was with Jack on the collapsible and recalled being "saved by the merest chance." He said survivors "on the lifeboat that rescued us hesitated . . . fearing perhaps that additional burdens would swamp the frail craft." Jack was so determined to get into Lifeboat 12 that he didn't notice his mother nearby in Lifeboat 4. Mrs. Thayer was so numbed by cold and shock that she did not see her son.

Jack's Rescue

More than six hours after Jack plunged into the sea, Lifeboat 12 arrived at the rescue ship, the *Carpathia*. Jack's mother was overjoyed to see her son. The *Carpathia*'s captain turned over his cabin to Mrs. Thayer, Mrs. Widener, and Mrs. John Jacob Astor. A kind passenger gave Jack some pajamas. For the next three nights, Jack slept on the floor of the captain's cabin, exhausted but alive.

STRIKES STARBOARD BOW -12 Ft. AFT — 11 45 P.M.

FORWARD END FLOATS THEN SINKS — 1 20 A.M.

SETTLES BY HEAD - BOATS ORDERED OUT — 12 05 A.M.

STERN SECTION. PIVOTS AMIDSHIPS AND SWINGS OVER SPOT WHERE FORWARD SECTION SANK — 2 00 A.M

SETTLES TO FORWARD STACK BREAKS BETWEEN STACKS — 1 40 A.M.

LAST POSITION IN WHICH TITANIC STAYED 5 MINUTES BEFORE THE FINAL PLUNGE

L. P. Skidmore. S.S. "Carpathia" Apr. 15th 1912.

While the rescue ship steamed toward New York, Jack described the sinking of the *Titanic* to *Carpathia* passenger L. P. Skidmore. Skidmore drew a series of pictures. Jack said the great ship split in two before it sank. For more than 70 years, people didn't believe Jack's description.

Before Jack died in 1945, his accounts of the ship, its sinking, and the rescue helped researchers put together the puzzle pieces of how the great *Titanic* sank.

SECOND ✦ CLASS

Second-class cabins had natural light, mahogany furniture, and bed curtains for privacy.

TITANIC

THE FINEST STEAMER IN THE WORLD

48,326 TONS

DECLARED "UNSINKABLE"

One Second Class Ticket to New York City, USA

E12

DEPARTING FROM SOUTHAMPTON
APRIL 10, 1912
With Stops in Cherbourg, France
And
Quee...

RUTH BECKER
Comforting Others

All Aboard for Second Class

With a loud screech, the boat train from London to the Southampton pier pulled up close to the *Titanic*. Twelve-year-old Ruth Becker, independent and sensible, yet adventurous, stepped off the train and boarded the ship towering above her.

Ruth, her mother, her younger sister, Marion, and little brother, Richard, had traveled by steamer halfway around the world. They had gone from India through the Suez Canal and the Mediterranean Sea to England. This ship was different—bigger, more elegant, and brand new. It would take them to the United States, where Richard could get medical treatment.

Strolling on the Boat Decks

To pass the time, Ruth pushed Richard in a stroller. Second-class passengers had an open boat deck to walk on. Nearby were the *Titanic*'s lifeboats, attached by cables to high cranes, called davits. But Ruth preferred to take Richard to the warmer enclosed deck intended for first-class passengers. There, she could peek through the windows into the first-class dining saloon. She later wrote, *I would look in the dining room and it was the most beautiful sight I ever saw . . . I just stood there and marveled, how beautiful everything was.*

t-class promenade deck.

Ruth Remains Calm

When the Beckers were ordered to evacuate the *Titanic* well past midnight on April 15, Ruth and her mother wore only coats over their nightgowns. But they dressed the younger children warmly. Waiting in a roomful of weeping women, Ruth stayed calm. "I was never scared. I was only excited. I never for one minute thought we would die," she said later.

Marion and Richard were handed into the overcrowded Lifeboat 11. Mrs. Becker begged to get in with her children. But there was no room for Ruth. She asked the officer in charge if she could take Lifeboat 13. The officer picked up Ruth and threw her in. When 65 people had filled the craft to its capacity, the cables were released. The lifeboat descended shakily down to the ocean.

Lifeboat 13

As it was being lowered, Ruth's lifeboat drifted directly underneath Lifeboat 15. If the craft above continued down, the passengers in Ruth's boat would be crushed. When Lifeboat 15 was only inches away, two seamen on Lifeboat 13 cut the ropes, freeing their craft so it could row out of harm's way.

Seated in the front, Ruth passed blankets to others. She gave her handkerchief to a crewman with a mangled finger. Always thinking of others, Ruth comforted an immigrant woman who had been separated from her family. The woman's tiny baby had been bundled up and handed into a different lifeboat. Ruth promised she would help the woman find her child.

When the *Carpathia* came to the rescue two hours later, Ruth's hands were so cold she could not grasp the ropes used to haul her up.

The Lucky Ones

Safely aboard the *Carpathia*, Ruth helped the woman find her baby. Then she found her own frantic mother. Many women and children were sobbing. Their husbands and fathers were missing. Ruth felt lucky—her own missionary father was safe in India.

Third class was also called steerage. Rooms like Anna's were the smallest on the *Titanic*, and steerage tickets were the cheapest. Still, the third-class cabins were roomy, with good quality wood paneling, warm floor coverings, and washbasins. The tables in the third-class dining room were covered in white linen tablecloths, and plenty of nourishing food was served.

As this poster shows, the *Titanic* was scheduled to return to England on April 20.

ANNA TURJA AND MINNIE COUTTS
Strangers in Steerage

Anna Turja

Looking for a New Life

Like many in the *Titanic*'s third class, 18-year-old Anna Turja left her home in Finland hoping to find work and a new life in America.

After Anna boarded in Southampton, England, the *Titanic* stopped in Cherbourg, France, to pick up more third-class passengers—Arabic-speakers from Syria, as well as families speaking Croatian, Armenian, Greek, and Lebanese. At dinner her second night, Anna heard many languages she did not understand, including English.

Other steerage passengers boarded the *Titanic* in Queenstown, Ireland. These Irish men and women were also joining relatives in the United States. For rich and poor, the *Titanic* was a "ship of dreams."

At dinner, Anna spoke Finnish with her cabinmates, Maria and Sanni. Maria's children were with her and perhaps played in the general room with the sons of Mrs. Minnie Coutts—Neville, age 3, and William, age 9. Minnie and her boys were sailing to join her husband, an engraver in New York.

Something "Like a Shudder"

Anna and her friends were in bed when the *Titanic* struck the iceberg. She was awakened by something that felt "like a shudder." She remembered thinking, *There is something wrong with the engines.*

The brother of one of her cabinmates alerted them: "Get up or soon you will be at the bottom of the ocean." Anna wasn't scared, but others fainted. Maria trembled as she dressed her sleepy children.

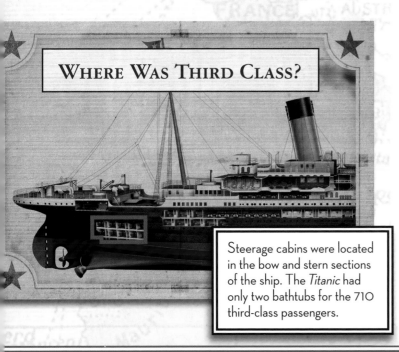

WHERE WAS THIRD CLASS?

Steerage cabins were located in the bow and stern sections of the ship. The *Titanic* had only two bathtubs for the 710 third-class passengers.

Minnie Waits and Wonders

In her cabin toward the rear of the ship, Minnie Coutts felt only a slight jolt. She lay awake for 15 minutes until she heard others outside her door.

She stepped into the hallway as passengers with suitcases moved toward the stern and up to an open rear deck. Most wore life jackets. Minnie didn't want to wake her sleeping sons, so she continued to wait for news.

Sitting on her bed, Minnie struggled not to panic. She had to set a good example for Neville and Willie. She waited nearly an hour in her room, allowing the boys to sleep.

Anna Disobeys Orders

Meanwhile, Anna and her friends made their way toward the boat deck. They disobeyed a seaman's orders to stop climbing up. After they passed, he closed and chained the doors behind them to prevent others from coming that way. Immigrants crowded together on the rear decks, which had no access to lifeboats.

Anna's group kept moving. "We were not told what had happened, and had to do our own thinking," she said. She called it "pure chance" that she emerged on the boat deck.

Minnie and Anna were berthed far apart because third-class cabins were spread over four different levels of the *Titanic*. Passengers had to navigate a maze of staircases, passageways, and decks to find their rooms.

Two large public rooms flanked either side of the main stairways leading down to the steerage cabins—a smoking room for men and a general room for all. There, third-class passengers talked, played cards, and read. Some played harmonicas, fiddles, Irish bagpipes, and small drums. Others sang or danced. Steerage passengers shared fun together, despite their language differences.

An American Angel Saves Minnie

Minnie realized she and her sons must evacuate, so she woke them up and tied their life vests on them. There wasn't a life vest for her.

She ran outside with the boys. Some passages were blocked, and Minnie found herself lost deep inside the ocean liner. Just when she had given up hope of finding her way, a seaman came along and said, "Hurry now; all women and children to the lifeboats."

Minnie later told the *Washington Post* that the seaman took the threesome to the side of the ship, where an American gentleman stepped up to her. He had heard Minnie asking for a life vest. The man raised his hat, and then slowly removed the life preserver he had strapped to himself.

"Take my life preserver, madam," he said. Then he reached over and put his hand on the children's heads. "If I go down, please pray for me."

Replica of a life vest from the *Titanic*.

Near Catastrophe in Two Lifeboats

Anna Turja left the *Titanic* in Lifeboat 15 at 1:40 a.m., two hours after the collision. Lifeboat 13, already in the water, had drifted under Anna's descending lifeboat. Ruth Becker looked up and saw the bottom of Lifeboat 15 heading toward her. Some men shouted, stood, and pushed against the boat above.

Quick-thinking crewmen found a knife and severed the ropes that had prevented Lifeboat 13 from moving away. They rowed it out of danger just in the nick of time. Ruth Becker and Anna Turja were safe in lifeboats. Jack Thayer was still aboard the *Titanic* as its stern lifted higher. Minnie Coutts was lining up with her boys for Lifeboat 2.

As Anna's lifeboat pulled away from the damaged ship, she heard explosions. The *Titanic*'s bright lights, which had been burning steadily since the collision, blinked out, leaving Anna in eerie darkness. Her lifeboat was close to the ship of dreams when it disappeared at 2:20 a.m.

Kindness Aboard the Carpathia

Minnie's boat was the first to be unloaded when the *Carpathia* arrived in the area at about 4:00 a.m. By about 9:00 a.m., all survivors were safely aboard. Anna and Minnie were met with great kindness. "There was no discrimination," Minnie said, "the poorest women receiving as much attention as the wealthiest."

When the *Carpathia* steamed in to New York Harbor on April 18, Minnie met her husband, and the boys were reunited with their father.

Anna Turja was taken to St. Vincent's Hospital. She had lost everything except her clothes. Others in her cabin did not survive. "I can never understand why God would have spared a poor Finnish girl when all those rich people drowned," Anna said.

Survivors aboard the *Carpathia*.

The Titanic's Female Crew

Violet and her roommate, Ann Turnbull, were two of just 23 women on the crew of the *Titanic*. Most of the *Titanic*'s female crew were stewardesses who worked long hours and catered to the wishes of the passengers to whom they were assigned. Bedroom stewardesses, like Violet, served tea, cleaned public rooms, and kept staterooms tidy. Two crew women were cashiers at the exclusive à la carte restaurant on B deck. One crew woman was a masseuse and another served as an attendant in the Turkish baths.

The cooling room of the *Titanic*'s Turkish baths. These were steam and heat treatment rooms that pampered wealthy passengers.

No. **529**

WHITE STAR LINE.

R.M.S. "TITANIC."

This ticket entitles bearer to use of Turkish or Electric Bath on one Occasion.

Paid 4/- or 1 Dollar.

Auburn-haired Violet Jessop was a favorite with White Star Line passengers and crew. She was young for a stewardess, and her good looks could distract male passengers. On one voyage, she received three marriage proposals.

VIOLET JESSOP
Super Survivor

Looking for Adventure

Twenty-four-year-old Violet Jessop, dressed in a new brown suit with an ankle-length skirt, rode through Southampton in a horse-drawn cab. It was her first day as a stewardess aboard RMS *Titanic*.

A few years before, Violet had been working on the White Star liner the *Olympic* when it collided with a British warship. Despite that accident, she liked the *Olympic*. Violet took the job on the *Titanic* because friends persuaded her it would be an adventure. After all, this was the new ship's first Atlantic crossing—its maiden voyage. Violet had no idea how much of an adventure she would encounter in the North Atlantic that April.

RMS *Olympic*.

A Walk Before Bed

[V]iolet liked to walk in the fresh air after her [w]orkday ended. And when it was time for [be]d, she was grateful that the ship's designer, [T]homas Andrews, had made the crew's [qu]arters so pleasant. She had a cozy bunk and [a] wardrobe in which to hang her clothes.

[O]n the fourth day out, she recalled, "A [l]ittle cold nip crept into the air as evening [s]et in." The chill emphasized the warmth and luxuriousness inside the ship. Upon settling down in her berth that night, Violet read aloud a Hebrew prayer that an old Irishwoman had given her. She asked Ann, her roommate, to also read aloud the words. Violet hoped the prayer would protect them from fire and water dangers. She was "comfortably drowsy" in her bunk, but not quite asleep when the collision occurred.

After the crash, Violet heard a "low, rending, crunching, ripping sound." Then silence.

Violet Saves a Life

Violet and Ann assisted passengers with their life belts and then proceeded to the boat deck. They watched "women cling to their husbands before being put into boats with their children." Later, both stewardesses were placed into Lifeboat 16.

As the lifeboat was being lowered, an officer called to Violet, "Look after this, will you?" With that, he dropped a bundled-up baby onto her lap. As the lifeboat was lowered down the side, Violet counted the decks by the rows of lights. "One, two, three, four, five, six; then again—one, two, three, four, five." She could no longer deny the truth in front of her: the *Titanic* was sinking.

Violet protected the child until the *Carpathia* arrived. Once aboard the rescue ship, a woman ran toward Violet, snatched the baby, and disappeared without saying a word.

Violet Sinks Again

Four years later, Violet was serving as a nurse on the White Star Line ship the *Britannic* (originally called the *Gigantic*), when it struck a mine near Greece and sank. Although she was injured and nearly drowned, once again Violet survived.

Dining at the Ritz

With a staff of 68, the à la carte restaurant, perhaps the finest in the world, outdid even the first-class dining saloon. Meals there were very expensive. Passengers called it the Ritz.

Luigi Gatti managed an international staff of waiters, roast cooks, pastry chefs, fish cooks, icemen, wine butlers, carvers, and platemen. Pageboys scurried about, carrying messages between tables.

The 1997 movie *Titanic* faithfully reproduced the look and feel of a first-class dinner party aboard the *Titanic*.

JACK PHILLIPS AND HAROLD BRIDE

Beyond the Call of Duty

Realistic re-creation of the Marconi room on the *Titanic*.

The Marconi Men

Jack Phillips and Harold Bride worked for the Marconi Company, named for the inventor of the new wireless telegraph. Jack, 25, was the *Titanic*'s senior wireless operator, and Harold, 22, was his assistant.

Operating the equipment in four-hour shifts, Harold and Jack took turns sleeping in a small bedroom next to the windowless office. The messages they sent and received were mostly between passengers.

Missed Messages

On Sunday afternoon, Harold and Jack were working feverishly to keep up with a backlog of messages. The wireless set had broken down the night before, and they were still catching up. At 1:40 p.m., a message arrived from another ship. It reported icebergs about 250 miles ahead of the *Titanic*. By 11:00 p.m., the *Titanic* had received seven iceberg warnings. Some were posted on the bridge, but not all of the messages were seen by Captain Smith.

Jack Phillips

Harold Bride

Calling for Help

At 11:40 that night, when the *Titanic*'s starboard bow struck a submerged iceberg, Harold and Jack sensed only minor damage. When the captain ordered them to send out the first distress call, Harold suggested that Jack should try the new *SOS* signal. "It may be your last chance," he joked. With a laugh, Jack switched from the traditional *CQD* signal to *SOS* in Morse code.

The SS *Californian* was only 20 miles away and could have come to the *Titanic*'s rescue, but the *Californian*'s wireless operator had signed off for the night. For unknown reasons, the *Californian*'s captain concluded the *Titanic*'s distress flares did not indicate serious trouble.

Harold and Jack realized the *Carpathia* was their only hope for rescue. The *Carpathia*'s captain heard their call and was moving at full steam toward the stricken *Titanic*—but it was at least four hours away.

Water Floods the Wireless Room

When Captain Smith realized the situation was hopeless, he released both men from duty. But Jack kept working. Harold went on deck to see how bad things were. He later wrote: *The water was pretty close up to the boat deck. There was a great scramble aft, and how poor Phillips worked through it I don't know. He was a brave man. . . . I suddenly felt for him a great reverence to see him standing there sticking to his work while everybody else was raging about. I will never live to forget the work of Phillips for the last awful fifteen minutes. . . . The boat deck was awash. Phillips clung on sending and sending.*

Swept Overboard

When water flooded their cabin, the men moved to A deck. There, Harold was swept off the deck with Collapsible B. He found himself underneath the overturned craft for what "seemed like a lifetime." Harold swam out from underneath the lifeboat and climbed on top. Jack Thayer, Officer Lightoller, and other freezing men eventually joined him. The surface of the craft became so crowded with survivors that they overlapped one another. Harold was in terrible pain because someone was sitting on his feet.

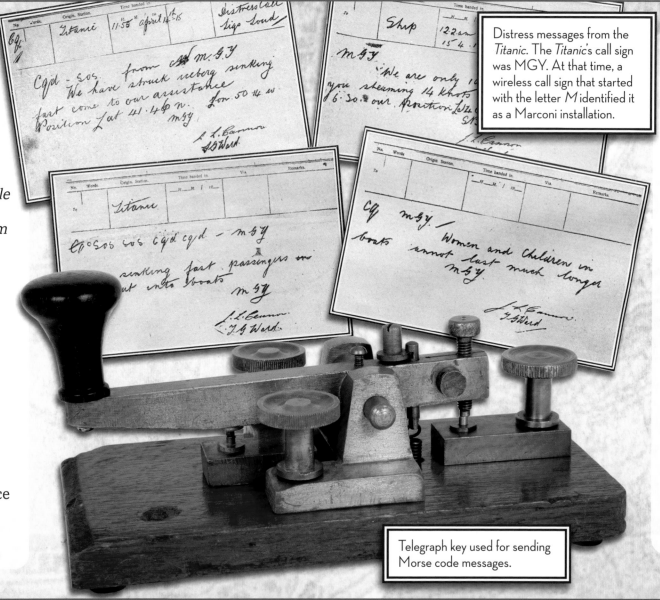

Distress messages from the *Titanic*. The *Titanic*'s call sign was MGY. At that time, a wireless call sign that started with the letter M identified it as a Marconi installation.

Telegraph key used for sending Morse code messages.

Watching the Titanic Go Down

Like Jack Thayer, Harold watched the ship go down: "There must have been an explosion, but we heard none," he later said. "The ship was gradually turning on her nose—just like a duck does that goes down for a dive."

Jack Phillips also made it to Collapsible B, but he died of exposure before they were rescued.

The Two Harolds

Aboard the *Carpathia*, Harold was taken first to the ship's hospital. Both of his feet were frostbitten and one was crushed. Hours later, Harold was carried to the wireless room. The sole wireless operator on the *Carpathia*, Harold Cottam, was a friend of Jack Phillips and Harold Bride. Together, the two Harolds began the task of transmitting the names of survivors to those who were waiting anxiously in New York.

The Age of Elegance

Technology, science, and society changed dramatically during the first two decades of the 20th century. This Edwardian era lasted from 1901 to 1919. Its name came from the popular English king, Edward VII. Some called these years the Age of Elegance. The opulence of the *Titanic* certainly reflected the times in which it was built.

The wireless telegraph, telephone, typewriter, electric lights, and even the bicycle were new inventions. The first airplane briefly flew in 1903, and travel by automobile became common. Human progress seemed unstoppable. Optimism and confidence were common themes.

In the Edwardian era, women's clothing showed a slimmer silhouette, but hats developed much wider brims. Wealthier women chose hats with feather decorations. Fur coats and stoles were also popular. Accessories included embroidered gloves, fancy parasols, and small, decorative handbags. Men wore suit coats, ties, gloves, gold watches, and hats, too.

THOMAS ANDREWS
The Titanic's *Creator Saves Others*

Thomas Andrews

The Terrible Truth

While Jack Phillips and Harold Bride were sending the first distress signals in the wireless room, Charles Lightoller and naval architect Thomas Andrews were trying to keep order on the boat deck.

The lifeboats had to be uncovered, swung out, and lowered even with the deck, so people could board them. Many passengers were reluctant to trade the warmth of the huge, well-lit ship for a tiny craft that was lowered by pulleys 50 feet into the dark, cold ocean.

The first lifeboat to be lowered, Lifeboat 7, touched the water at about 12:45 a.m., about an hour after the *Titanic*'s run-in with the iceberg. Captain Smith, his officers, most of the crew, and architect Andrews already knew the terrible truth. If the *Titanic* sank, not everyone could be saved. The ship carried more than 2,200 passengers. Fully loaded, the 16 regular lifeboats plus the four with collapsible sides could carry fewer than 1,200.

Even so, there were only 25 people aboard Lifeboat 7. The lifeboat could hold 65.

Lifeboats and davits on the boat deck of the *Titanic*'s sister ship, the *Olympic*.

"Our Beloved Designer"

Thomas Andrews had helped design the great ship. He was well liked by its staff, especially Violet Jessop. She wrote that during the first four days, "our beloved designer" went about *with a tired face but a satisfied air. He never failed to stop for a cheerful word, his only regret that we were getting further from home.*

When Andrews knew his own creation was doomed, he did everything he could to get passengers to safety. After the collision, stewardess May Sloan said Andrews looked heartbroken when he told her the situation. He asked her to downplay the danger to maintain calm. He told his steward, Henry Etches, to instruct passengers to dress warmly and to find the life preservers stowed on top of their wardrobes.

The Final Minutes

As the *Titanic* dipped farther into the water, passengers became more nervous. The lifeboats that left later, such as Ruth Becker's, were fully loaded. By 2:05 a.m., the ship's entire bow was underwater, and all but two lifeboats had been launched.

As the ship sank, Officer Lightoller dove off the top and was sucked underwater against one of the *Titanic*'s massive funnels. He struggled to safety aboard the upside-down Collapsible B with Harold Bride and Jack Thayer.

The heartbroken Thomas Andrews was last seen staring at the painting, *The Approach to Plymouth Harbour,* that hung above the fireplace in the first-class smoking room. His family in Ireland later received a telegram quoting survivors in New York: INTERVIEW *TITANIC*'S OFFICERS. ALL UNANIMOUS ANDREWS HEROIC UNTO DEATH, THINKING ONLY SAFETY OTHERS.

BRAVE WOMEN IN THE LIFEBOATS

High-Spirited Molly Brown

Known by her nickname Molly, Margaret Tobin Brown boarded the *Titanic* at Cherbourg, France. She was returning home to America after a trip to Egypt. Unlike the sedate wives of many wealthy Americans, Molly was high-spirited and openhearted. Those traits made her independent, but many in the straitlaced first-class section shunned her. Molly was traveling without her husband, a Denver mining millionaire.

After spending the evening with John Jacob Astor IV and his young bride, Molly was getting ready for bed. Stewards brought word that she should don a life jacket and go up to the boat deck. Officer Lightoller pointed her toward Lifeboat 6, which was launched at 12:55 a.m. But when Molly turned away to see what was happening elsewhere on the deck, the lifeboat began lowering without her. "You are going, too!" a crewman growled, grabbing the stout woman and dropping her four feet down into the boat. Also aboard were Lookout Frederick Fleet and Quartermaster Robert Hichens. Hichens was put in charge.

Drama in Lifeboat 6

As the boat was slowly lowered, Lightoller had second thoughts about the small crew of two men. He called for another man to come aboard to help row. Canadian Major Arthur Peuchen, an experienced yachtsman, volunteered. He bravely swung hand over hand down the ropes leading to the waiting lifeboat below.

Only 24 people were aboard Lifeboat 6, although it could hold 65. Hichens curtly told those who wanted to go back to rescue others, "It is our lives now, not theirs." He feared the craft would be swamped if they hauled people floating nearby aboard.

Molly Brown

The Countess in Lifeboat 8

In Lifeboat 8, Noëlle Leslie, the privileged Countess of Rothes, handled the tiller strongly and well. The tiller is a steering bar that turns the rudder beneath a boat to the left or right. Along with two other women and Seaman Thomas Jones, the countess wanted to row back to rescue people who were floundering in the freezing water. But the majority in the underfilled lifeboat overruled those who wanted to turn back. "Ladies, if any of us are saved, remember I wanted to go back. I would rather drown with them than leave them," Seaman Jones said.

Later, the countess moved to sit next to a weeping newlywed whose husband remained aboard the *Titanic*. Staying near the grieving girl, the countess picked up an oar and rowed the lifeboat until morning. After they were rescued, Seaman Jones had the number *8* from their lifeboat mounted on a plaque. He presented it to the countess and thanked her for her help that grim night.

Noëlle Leslie,
Countess of Rothes

Lifeboat with man standing at the tiller.

Women and Children Only!

First Officer Murdoch was in charge of the starboard lifeboats. He allowed men into the boats with their wives and families or if there were no women or children nearby. When Second Officer Lightoller took over on the port side, he followed the "women and children only" motto. Lightoller put only women and children into the boats, even if there were empty seats.

At a Senate inquiry into the disaster, Senator William A. Smith of Michigan asked Lightoller if he had followed the "women and children only" rule because of the captain's orders or "the rule of the sea." Lightoller replied that he had done so because of "the rule of human nature."

Charles Lightoller

Molly Brown Takes Charge

Quartermaster Hichens was cruel and insensitive during their fearsome night at sea. He yelled at the crewman who was rowing. He implied that Fleet's poor performance would leave them drifting in the North Atlantic.

Infuriated by Hichens's negative remarks, Molly told him he should hand over the tiller to a woman and row himself. When he refused, Molly placed an oar in an oarlock and began rowing. So did Margaret Martin, the second cashier at the ship's à la carte restaurant.

Molly encouraged other women to do the same. She taught them how to pull the oar smoothly through the water in a steady rhythm.

For safety, Hichens ordered Lifeboat 6 to tie up with Lifeboat 16. Later, as Margaret Martin was pulling on one of the oars, she thought she saw a light on the horizon. She called it a "flash of lightning." Hichens contradicted her: "It is a falling star," he said. But they were both wrong. It was the *Carpathia*. Though the rescue ship was still at a distance, its lights were visible on the horizon—and the vessel was moving closer.

Years before boarding the *Titanic*, Helen Churchill Candee wrote a book for women who worked to support themselves—this was unusual in the early 1900s. Although she was injured in the *Titanic* disaster, Helen continued to travel and to write books that inspired women to rely on their own resources. As a suffragette, she worked to give women the right to vote.

Helen Candee

Maintaining Hope

During the long night, Molly Brown cheered on the female rowers. When the *Carpathia* came into view of her lifeboat, she wanted to row toward it. Hichens again reacted negatively. Under his order, Lifeboats 6 and 16 had been drifting. When a passenger asked him if the ship in the distance was coming to their rescue, he replied, "No, she is not going to pick us up."

Molly Brown and the other women, including the feminist author Helen Candee, would not allow Hichens to prevent them from being saved. Molly wrapped her fur stole around the legs of one shivering man and ordered another half-frozen man to row. The exercise would warm him. Molly also demanded that the two boats be cut apart. When Hichens protested, she threatened to throw him overboard.

With Hichens cowering at the tiller, Molly took charge and Lifeboat 6 rowed toward the *Carpathia*.

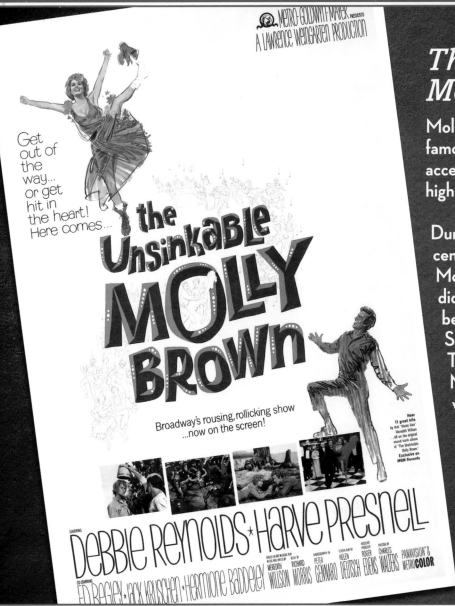

The Unsinkable Molly Brown

Molly's bold actions made her briefly famous. After the sinking, she was accepted, at least for a short time, by high society in Denver.

During the first decades of the 20th century, American women could not vote. Molly and the other brave women who did a "man's job" in the lifeboats became beacons for the early feminist movement. Suffragettes praised their courage. The actions of female survivors like Molly Brown were cited as evidence of women's full equality with men.

Molly's greatest fame came later, after she died. In 1960 she was the subject of a Broadway musical, *The Unsinkable Molly Brown*. Four years later, the musical became a movie.

Learning to Row in Lifeboat 2

Mrs. Mahala Douglas of Minneapolis was seated near the tiller in Lifeboat 2. Few in that boat knew how to row. Members of the *Titanic*'s crew had spent their adult lives working on steamships, and they did not have experience rowing. *When we were finally launched*, she wrote in a letter later, *the rowing was very difficult, for no one knew how. I tried to steer, under Mr. Boxhall's orders, and he put the lantern—an old one, with very little light in it—on a pole. A bit later*, she reported, *we stopped rowing to listen for the lapping of the water against the icebergs.*

Shortly after 4:00 a.m., as the *Carpathia* coasted toward Lifeboat 2, Mrs. Douglas shouted up to the rescue ship, "The *Titanic* has gone down with everyone on board!"

Mahala Douglas

THE TITANIC WITH LIFEBOATS DEPLOYED

The Mail Room

The initials *RMS* on a British ship meant "Royal Mail Ship." Mail ships carried mail from continent to continent.

The mail room on RMS *Titanic*'s G deck held hundreds of mail sacks. One deck higher, a post office served passengers and crew. Five postal workers sorted nearly half a million letters on their way to New York and beyond.

Mailbags being carried on board.

POST CARD

Place Stamp Here

Place Stamp Here

Domestic One cent

Foreign Two cents

HEROES WHO STAYED BEHIND

Saving the Mail

In addition to passengers, RMS *Titanic* was carrying an estimated 400,000 pieces of mail from England to the United States. Shortly after the collision, Fourth Officer Joseph Boxhall was inspecting the ship when a postal worker alerted him that the vessel was taking on water. "The mail hold is filling rapidly!" the clerk cried.

The mail room was located deep in the bow of the ship. After the collision, it flooded quickly. Already, four clerks, standing knee-deep in water, were desperately trying to pull 200 sacks of registered mail from G deck to the higher F deck. The clerks asked a steward to help them haul the heavy bags. When the steward urged the clerks to leave their posts, the postal workers shook their heads and continued their work. They were last seen dragging mail sacks up the stairways in an effort to keep the mail dry. All five men were lost in the Atlantic that night.

Calming Passengers with Music

To calm passengers that frightening night, bandleader Wallace Hartley quickly pulled together the *Titanic*'s two instrumental groups: his quintet and a trio that played cello, violin, and piano. The newly assembled eight-member orchestra played cheerful ragtime tunes in the first-class lounge. They later moved to the boat deck. Passengers waiting to board lifeboats, like Anna Turja, were struck by how the music calmed frightened women and children.

As the ship's bow sank lower, Hartley changed the mood of the music. From 12:15 to 2:00 a.m., when the tilt of the *Titanic* made holding cellos, violins, and other instruments nearly impossible, the musicians played on.

Survivors remembered the comfort the gift of music provided. None of the eight musicians attempted to board a lifeboat. All perished.

There were no more boats, water was swirling around the upper deck, people were beginning to panic . . . and the band continued to play. —Helen Churchill Candee

"Where You Go, I Go."

While the lifeboats were being loaded and the music played, a famous couple from New York approached Lifeboat 8. Isidor Straus was co-owner of Macy's department store and had been a member of the U.S. Congress. His wife, Ida, was at his side.

The Strauses had been married for more than 40 years and had seven children. The officer loading the lifeboat wanted to allow 67-year-old Isidor to board with his wife. But Isidor refused. He said younger men and his wife's maid, Ellen Bird, should enter the lifeboat first.

After Ellen boarded, Ida Straus handed her maid a blanket, but she didn't get into the lifeboat. She turned to her husband and said, "We have been living together for many years and where you go, I go."

Friends urged Ida to seek safety with the women in the lifeboat. "No," she said. "I will not be separated from my husband." Lifeboat 8 left at 1:10 a.m. without the Strauses. Later, Officer Lightoller saw the couple and offered to take Ida to one of the remaining lifeboats. "I think I'll stay here for the present," Mrs. Straus answered politely and calmly.

Her husband urged her again; once more, she refused. The Strauses moved to a deck bench and sat down together. Ida was last seen seated next to her husband, the two embracing to the end as the ship sank into the frigid waters of the North Atlantic.

Seven members of the *Titanic's* band.

Isidor and Ida Straus

A Journalist and Prophet

William Thomas Stead earned fame as a journalist in England. He pioneered what is now called investigative journalism. Working hard and taking risks, he dug deep into records to expose injustice.

Stead was traveling to the United States on the *Titanic* for a peace conference. President William Howard Taft had asked him to attend the event.

After the ship struck the iceberg, Stead helped women and children board lifeboats. He was last seen calmly reading in the first-class smoking room.

William Stead

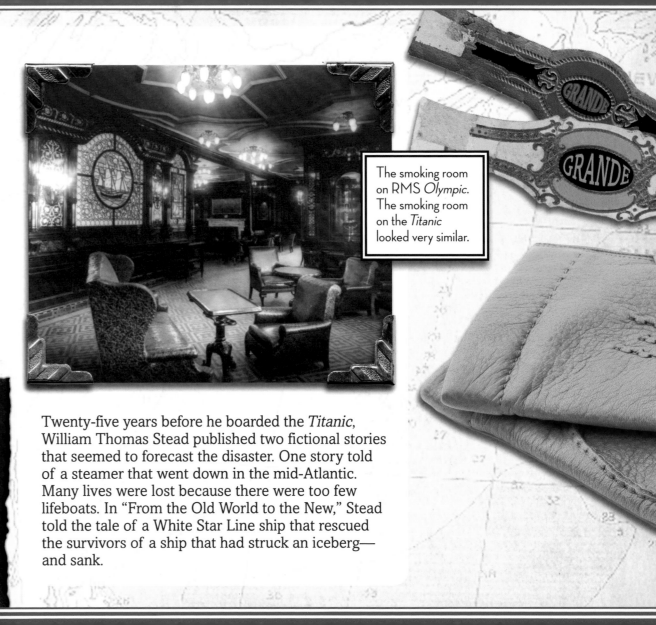

The smoking room on RMS *Olympic*. The smoking room on the *Titanic* looked very similar.

Hypothermia

Most of those in the water died from a form of exposure called hypothermia. Their internal body temperatures became too low to support basic body functions. They shivered, grew pale and sleepy, and their breathing and heartbeat gradually slowed down. As one *Titanic* researcher wrote, *Death from hypothermia comes gently . . . Most of the Titanic's lost souls slipped into their final sleep within several minutes of entering the freezing ocean.*

Twenty-five years before he boarded the *Titanic*, William Thomas Stead published two fictional stories that seemed to forecast the disaster. One story told of a steamer that went down in the mid-Atlantic. Many lives were lost because there were too few lifeboats. In "From the Old World to the New," Stead told the tale of a White Star Line ship that rescued the survivors of a ship that had struck an iceberg—and sank.

A Gallant Gentleman

John Jacob Astor IV was the wealthiest man aboard the *Titanic* and one of the wealthiest men in America. He accompanied his pregnant young wife to A deck, where Officer Lightoller was boarding first-class women and children through windows into Lifeboat 4. Astor asked if he could go with his wife to protect her, but Lightoller would not make an exception to his "women and children only" rule. Despite his immense wealth and power, Colonel Astor obeyed. He gallantly stepped back, tossed his wife his gloves, and died in the sinking.

Madeleine Astor

John Jacob Astor

Captain Edward J. Smith

Down with His Ship

In some of the most dramatic testimony given after the disaster, wireless operator Harold Bride told a haunting story of the last seconds of Captain Smith's life. From his awkward perch on the overturned collapsible, Bride caught sight of Captain Smith, a solitary figure on the bridge of the *Titanic*. Wearing no life preserver, the captain dove overboard from the bridge into the icy waters. He was obeying the unwritten law of the sea—a captain must go down with his ship.

HEROES TO THE END

Loyal crew members, like the mail clerks and the band members, and hundreds of honorable passengers, from millionaires to immigrants, faced death with great courage. These men—and women such as Ida Straus—showed the strong sense of duty and confidence that were hallmarks of the Edwardian era. They were heroes to the end.

ARTHUR ROSTRON
The Carpathia *and Its Brave Captain*

The "Electric Spark"

At 12:35 a.m. on April 15, RMS *Carpathia*'s wireless operator, Harold Cottam, burst into the captain's cabin. He carried news of the *Titanic*'s distress call. The *Carpathia* was sailing from New York to Europe. Captain Arthur Rostron rose quickly from his bed and wired back his position. He promised that the *Carpathia* would come to the stricken ship's rescue.

The captain ordered his steamer to move at top speed, and he posted additional lookouts on the bow to watch for ice. Rostron's nickname was "Electric Spark." Already his energy, eagerness, and good instincts were driving him forward.

Full Speed Ahead!

Rostron and his crew would interrupt a pleasant spring cruise to the Mediterranean to launch the rescue mission. They could only plan and hope to reach the *Titanic* in time. The two ships were about 58 miles apart. With a usual top speed of 14 knots, closing the distance would take nearly four hours. Captain Rostron ordered the heating and other systems shut down. All the steam generated had to be used to move the ship. Soon, the *Carpathia* was dodging icebergs and racing at a speed of more than 17 knots!

RMS *Carpathia*, a Cunard ship, was much smaller than the *Titanic*.

The Carpathia Prepares for Rescue

Captain Rostron ordered the ship's three doctors to prepare each of the three dining rooms with supplies to treat the injured. Stewards brewed coffee for the crew. They prepared warm drinks and secured blankets for those rescued. The captain knew that stewards would have to calm his own 743 passengers and keep them apart from the rescue operations. Stewards would also be expected to console survivors.

The experienced seaman knew the risks and dangers of rescue efforts. Ropes, sling chairs, leather bags, and ladders were all readied to lift survivors from the waters or from lifeboats. The *Carpathia* was still 40 miles from the *Titanic* when its wireless operator received the message of doom from the other ship. It read: *Engine room getting flooded.*

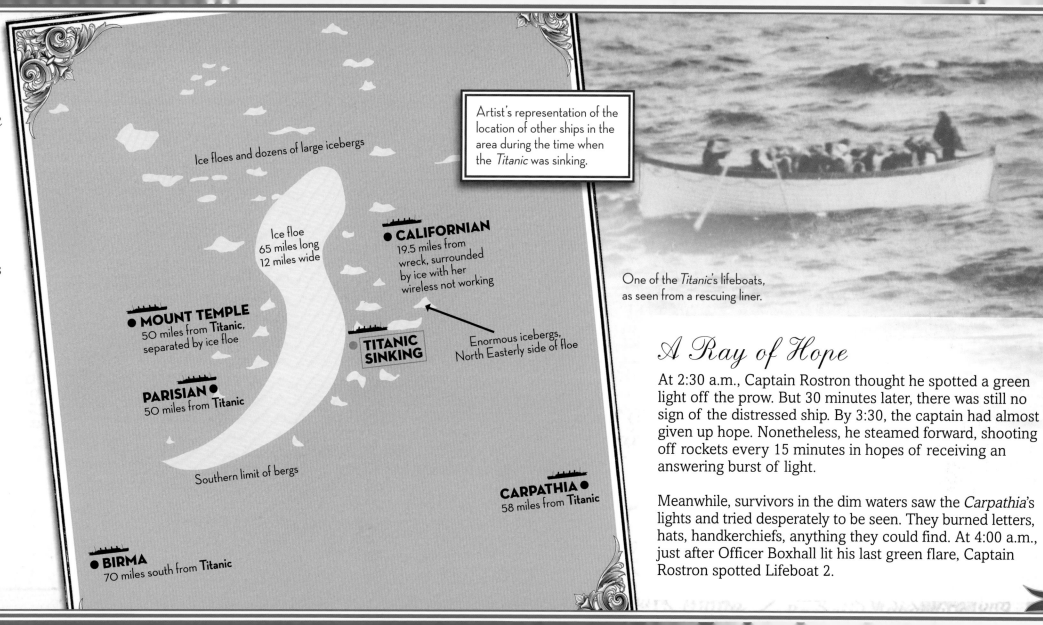

Ice floes and dozens of large icebergs

Artist's representation of the location of other ships in the area during the time when the *Titanic* was sinking.

Ice floe
65 miles long
12 miles wide

CALIFORNIAN
19.5 miles from wreck, surrounded by ice with her wireless not working

MOUNT TEMPLE
50 miles from *Titanic*, separated by ice floe

TITANIC SINKING

Enormous icebergs, North Easterly side of floe

PARISIAN
50 miles from *Titanic*

Southern limit of bergs

CARPATHIA
58 miles from *Titanic*

BIRMA
70 miles south from *Titanic*

One of the *Titanic*'s lifeboats, as seen from a rescuing liner.

A Ray of Hope

At 2:30 a.m., Captain Rostron thought he spotted a green light off the prow. But 30 minutes later, there was still no sign of the distressed ship. By 3:30, the captain had almost given up hope. Nonetheless, he steamed forward, shooting off rockets every 15 minutes in hopes of receiving an answering burst of light.

Meanwhile, survivors in the dim waters saw the *Carpathia*'s lights and tried desperately to be seen. They burned letters, hats, handkerchiefs, anything they could find. At 4:00 a.m., just after Officer Boxhall lit his last green flare, Captain Rostron spotted Lifeboat 2.

Lifeboat 2 Is Rescued

"Shut down your engines and take us aboard!" Officer Boxhall called up to the *Carpathia*. The steamer was soon alongside the small craft. A rope ladder was lowered to rescue the relieved occupants.

Boxhall was the last to leave the lifeboat. When he was brought to the captain on the bridge, Rostron asked if the *Titanic* had gone down. Boxhall told him it had. Rostron asked if there were many people left on board when she sank.

"Hundreds and hundreds! Perhaps a thousand!" Boxhall cried. As he grew more emotional, the captain invited him to go below for some hot coffee. The enormous scale of the disaster was becoming clear.

A rope ladder is lowered from the *Carpathia* to one of the *Titanic's* lifeboats.

The Carpathia Keeps Searching

Smoking from her one funnel, the *Carpathia* searched for other survivors. Some in the lifeboats despaired of being seen. Lifeboat 1, with its dozen occupants, was the next to be rescued. One by one, the heavier boats slowly approached, along with those that had been lashed together during the night.

Dawn was breaking as Lifeboat 14 approached the *Carpathia,* towing the nearly swamped Collapsible D. Eva Hart, age 7, and other children were winched up to the *Carpathia* inside heavy sacks. They were too small to climb the rope ladders. Eva said the experience was "terrifying, swinging about over the ocean." Even adult survivors needed help. A safety rope was slung under each person's shoulders so no one would fall back into the water.

Eva Hart

Collapsible D

Captain Rostron with *Carpathia* passenger Marjory Sweetheart. She gave all her spare clothes to children who were rescued from the *Titanic*.

The Last Lifeboat

Nearly four hours after the rescue operation began, Officer Lightoller struggled to guide Lifeboat 12 close to the rescue ship. Crowded with 75 people, the little boat dipped low in the water. It risked foundering in the rough sea. But at 8:30 a.m., the last lifeboat found shelter near the *Carpathia*, which saved every single person.

In all, 705 *Titanic* survivors were brought aboard the *Carpathia*.

Assessing the Scene

Captain Rostron saw that a number of the lifeboats weren't full. He noted, too, that many of the passengers were not warmly or fully clothed. Clearly, they had evacuated the *Titanic* in a hurry.

The White Star Line's managing director, Bruce Ismay, was in a state of shock. He shut himself up in a doctor's cabin. Panicked women worried about their missing husbands. Children wondered about their fathers. All the while, the *Carpathia*'s crew members treated everyone with respect and care.

The Carpathia Heads to New York

After surveying the area one last time, Captain Rostron lowered the flag to half-mast and held two prayer services. He gave thanks for the survival of so many and offered a funeral service for the more than 1,500 dead.

At 8:50 a.m. on Monday, April 15, Captain Rostron fired the engines and moved away to take the survivors to their original destination, New York. At first, he found his way blocked by ice. These were the same icebergs described by a warning that never reached the *Titanic*'s Captain Smith.

Survivors aboard the *Carpathia*.

Immigrants and Ellis Island

The majority of passengers in steerage were immigrants. Like Anna Turja, they boarded the *Titanic* seeking better lives in America. Of 710 third-class passengers, only 174 survived.

Immigrants were typically dropped off at Ellis Island in New York Harbor. This was a processing center near the Statue of Liberty. At Ellis Island, immigrants were asked questions to determine whether they met the requirements to come into the United States. Because they had already suffered so much, *Titanic* immigrants were allowed to leave the ship without going through the processing center.

Immigrant aid societies met many newcomers and offered clothing, money, and train tickets. Newspapers ran stories asking people to help. Already poor, immigrant survivors were left with nothing. Two traveled from New York to Chicago wearing just nightgowns beneath their coats.

THE SURVIVORS ARRIVE IN NEW YORK

The Biggest News of the Year

In New York City, 30,000 people gathered in the rain and cold to wait for the *Carpathia*. Relatives, journalists, the curious—all wanted to know what happened and who survived. The sinking of the "unsinkable" *Titanic* was the biggest news of the year.

As Captain Rostron brought the *Carpathia* into New York Harbor, an awesome sight greeted Ruth Becker. Yachts, tugboats, and smaller craft surrounded the steamer. Some had been leased by newspapers. Reporters were shouting questions to survivors through megaphones. The New York police force was there to hold back the crowds when the *Carpathia* docked. It was 9:00 p.m. on Thursday, April 18.

Leaving the Ship

Ruth Becker walked down the *Carpathia*'s gangway with her family. She was wearing a blanket for a skirt. Photographers with bright lights snapped photos. Although huge spotlights lit the pier, it was hard for the Beckers to find their friends.

Harold Bride's feet were so damaged that he had to be carried from the rescue ship. Many others needed to be helped down the gangway. Joyous greetings mixed with sobs of grief.

Confusion soon turned to chaos as friends and relatives called out for survivors. The *Titanic* passengers tried but sometimes failed to meet those waiting for them. Some immigrants melted into the crowds without checking in with authorities.

A crowd of people waiting for survivors.

Harold Bride being carried off the *Carpathia*.

Ismay and Others Detained

Also waiting at Pier 54 for the *Carpathia*'s arrival were two U.S. senators with a subpoena for the White Star Line's Bruce Ismay. Dozens of crew members and survivors from first, second, and third class were told to stay in New York for the official hearings about the disaster.

The Survivors Go Home

Harold Bride was taken to the home of his uncle on West 92nd Street. Harold Cottam, the wireless operator from the *Carpathia*, went with him. A *New York Times* reporter visited and found Bride, still with both feet in bandages. The newspaper sent messages back to England for him. One went to Harold's mother, another to the nurse he was going to marry.

Cottam also sent a telegram to his mother. *Am safe and well*, it read. *Detained in New York for Senatorial investigation.*

Nellie Becker and her children soon left New York by train for Benton Harbor, Michigan. Ruth's father joined them from India the next year. Little Eva Hart and her mother stayed in New York just long enough to buy tickets back to England.

Jack Thayer returned with his mother to their home in Haverford, outside Philadelphia, Pennsylvania. Like so many who arrived in New York that night, his life would be haunted by the disaster.

SENATOR WILLIAM A. SMITH
Safer Travel by Sea

Survivors Tell Their Stories

Just one day after the *Carpathia* reached New York, the U.S. Senate opened hearings into the disaster. Senator William A. Smith traveled from Washington, D.C., to New York to take testimony. At the Waldorf-Astoria Hotel, a chandelier glittered in the ballroom. The hearing room was nearly as fancy as the first-class dining saloon of the *Titanic*.

Americans were hungry to know what happened. Newspapers and radio covered the hearings extensively. Interest grew as people realized the scope of the disaster.

Bruce Ismay

The Waldorf-Astoria Hotel in New York City.

Ismay Is Called First

Senators called Bruce Ismay to testify first. He seemed to know little about iceberg warnings and the wireless operators. He said the *Titanic* had legal permission to leave England without enou lifeboats for all passengers. Those facts surprised the senators.

Because Ismay had escaped the *Titanic* before any senior office some called him a coward. Others unfairly blamed him and his company for the tragedy. People on both sides of the Atlantic wanted answers. Ismay was an easy target.

Captain Rostron Testifies

Captain Rostron testified next. He told of his immediate decision to come to the *Titanic*'s rescue. He listed his orders that night and stressed "the necessity for order, discipline, and quietness, and to avoid all confusion."

As dawn broke, Rostron said, he could see all the remaining *Titanic* lifeboats. But he also saw "about 20 icebergs . . . from 150 to 200 feet high and numerous smaller bergs." It became clear that the brave captain had taken tremendous risks to rescue the survivors of the *Titanic*.

Molly Brown presents a trophy to Captain Rostron, thanking him for his bravery.

Harold Bride's Astonishing Story

On the second day, wireless operator Harold Bride arrived in a wheelchair to testify. His account of distress calls, frantic messages, and misunderstandings shocked the onlookers. Reporters said Harold recounted "one of the most astonishing sea stories ever told." Details of the drama on Collapsible B were in all the newspapers.

Testaments of Courage

When Officer Lightoller was called, he admitted underfilling lifeboats at first because he wasn't sure how much weight each could carry. He said he had a hard time finding enough women and children to fill them. And he told his harrowing story of diving into the icy water and nearly drowning. Again, listeners heard the story of Collapsible B.

Frederick Fleet recalled his fateful shout from the crow's nest, "Iceberg right ahead!" Major Peuchen, from Molly Brown's lifeboat, testified: "I did not see a cowardly act by any man."

Some testimony conflicted. Some reports were later proved untrue. Still, key details, characters, and answers about the *Titanic*'s sinking emerged over 18 days. By the end of May, the Senate Committee issued its report.

The Titanic's Legal Legacy

There were no prosecutions or trials. In 1912, few laws governed travel and shipping by sea. No laws had been broken. Two of the star witnesses were "Marconi man" Harold Bride and Officer Lightoller. Their testimonies led Congress to pass important new safety legislation for passenger liners:

- Every ship must have a lifeboat seat and a life vest for each person aboard.
- Everyone aboard must participate in at least one lifeboat drill to practice evacuation procedures.
- There must be a 24-hour radio watch. That means every ship's crew must have enough wireless operators for round-the-clock transmissions.
- Later, in 1914, the U.S. Coast Guard created the International Ice Patrol. These officers find, note, and track the movement of ice fields in the Northwest Atlantic. They also conduct a *Titanic* memorial service each year on April 15.

THE TITANIC FOUND: JACK THAYER WAS RIGHT

Dreams of Finding the Titanic

As early as 1914, dreamers schemed to find the *Titanic* and raise it in one piece.

Some imagined lifting the wreck by attaching helium-filled bags to the hull. Others wanted to fill the ship with Ping-Pong balls. More practically, oceanographers hoped to find and perhaps take photographs of the lost ship.

Yet the final resting place of the *Titanic* remained a mystery. Its condition was unknown. More than two miles beneath the surface, the ship of dreams lay at the bottom of the sea, silent.

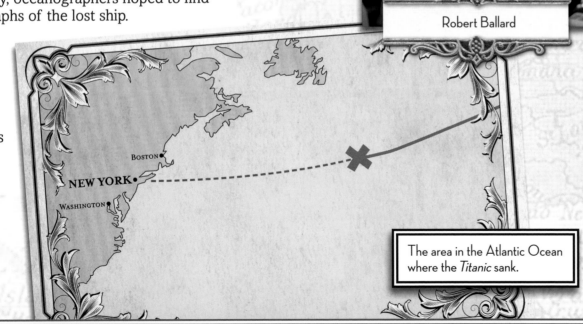

The area in the Atlantic Ocean where the *Titanic* sank.

Robert Ballard

Robert Ballard Discovers the Titanic

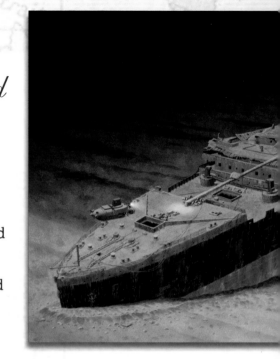

Early attempts to find the ship failed. Then, in 1985, the American underwater geologist Robert Ballard used new inventions to conduct a search. He had a camera sled and a remotely operated vehicle (ROV) called *Argo*. Ballard dragged *Argo* over a wide arc of the ocean floor.

On September 1, *Argo* found a debris field. The scientists guessed they had found the *Titanic* when the underwater camera focused on a large round object. It looked like one of the *Titanic*'s enormous boilers—and it was!

The scientists also realized the ship was split into two large pieces more than 600 yards apart. The pieces faced in opposite directions. Jack Thayer had been right! The *Titanic* broke in two before it sank.

The bow of the *Titanic*.

Painting of a submarine inspecting the *Titanic* as it rests on the seafloor. The two sections of the ship are widely separated, with a debris field between them.

Touring the Titanic

The following year, Ballard and two other scientists descended from the surface in *Alvin*, a small submarine. The ride down into the sea lasted two and a half hours.

Then we saw it, Ballard wrote. Titanic'*s black steel skin seemed to stretch into infinity.*

On subsequent dives, they saw the ship's bow and its grand staircase. The team's ROV captured photos of the elegance that once graced the *Titanic*.

Objects that had settled in the debris field between the two parts of the ship included a footboard from a first-class bed like Jack Thayer's, sinks like Ruth Becker's, and even a bathtub.

Ballard and his scientists respected these items as relics of lost human beings. They saw the *Titanic* as an underwater graveyard.

Au gratin dishes from the *Titanic*, which settled onto the seafloor without breaking.

Treasure Hunters and Titanic's Future

Other explorers and treasure hunters, who came later, were less respectful than Ballard's team. They removed items from the ship and the debris field. Nearly 2,000 objects from the ship have been brought to the surface for display.

Recent discoveries of a metal-eating bacteria that threatens to turn the *Titanic* into a pile of dust will only intensify the debate over what should be done with the wreckage.

THE TITANIC LIVES ON

A Hundred Years of Inspiration

For a hundred years, the doomed *Titanic* has inspired stories, paintings, histories, and films.

Just a month after the sinking, survivor Dorothy Gibson starred in a silent film about the disaster. In the film, she wore the same water-stained dress she had on the night she was rescued. Other movies and plays followed. James Cameron's 1997 Academy Award–winning film, *Titanic,* which features footage of the sunken wreckage, kindled new interest in the *Titanic.*

Soon after the disaster, memorials sprang up around the world. The grandest *Titanic* memorial was built with a gift from Eleanor Widener to honor her son, Harry. The Widener Library is the flagship library at Harvard University in Cambridge, Massachusetts. After talking with Jack Thayer that fateful night on the *Titanic,* Harry perished along with his father. Mrs. Widener built the library in her son's name. It now has 50 miles of shelves filled with three million books!

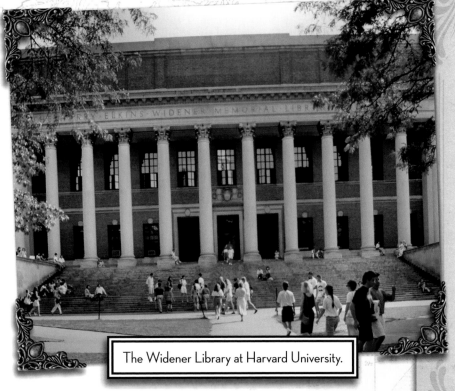

The Widener Library at Harvard University.

HEROES OF THE TITANIC

On that cold, still April night in 1912, more than 2,200 people faced a terrible crisis. Passengers such as Ruth Becker, Jack Thayer, Violet Jessop, and Molly Brown stayed calm, helped others, and acted bravely. The Strauses, Thomas Andrews, members of the band, the mail clerks, and others did what they believed was their duty.

These heroes survive in memory and legend to remind us of human nature at its best. Their courage inspires us to ask ourselves hard questions: How would I behave if I had to face the same peril? What life-or-death choices might I have made on that clear, starlit night?

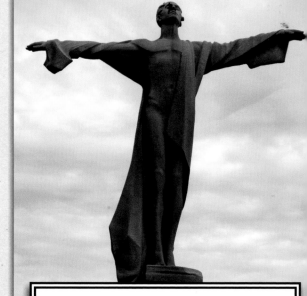

The *Titanic* Memorial in Washington, D.C., was erected by the Women's *Titanic* Memorial Association to honor the men who gave up their lives so that women and children might be saved.